The Penguin

Story by
ANGELA SHEEHAN

Pictures by
TREVOR BOYER

WARWICK PRESS

Through the clear, cold water, the penguin glimpsed a shoal of shiny blue fish and dived after them. With one gulp, he swallowed a tasty fish. Then he rose to the surface for a mouthful of air and dived again for more fish. When he had eaten his fill he swam out to sea, twisting and turning like a playful dolphin.

But he did not play for long. There was danger in the water. A vast killer whale had loomed up, his gaping mouth hungry for a victim. The penguin turned and swam for his life. He could feel the whale's mighty body lashing the water behind him, as he dodged its cruel teeth.

At last the penguin reached the ice. As the whale's jaws snapped, he leapt high out of the water to safety.

Tired from the chase, the penguin fell asleep. He slept standing on the ice, ready to wake at the slightest danger. But there were no dangers, only a few other penguins and vast stretches of ice.

But far in the distance, there were many more penguins. So the penguin set out to find them. All over the ice, there were penguins heading for the same place. After days of walking and resting, the penguin heard the cries. Hundreds of penguins stood chattering on the ice.

They seemed too busy to take any notice of him. He waddled here and there, making long loud calls to let the other penguins know he had arrived. But none of them looked up. So he stood a little way away from the crowd and turned his head proudly from side to side.

The bright orange feathers on his neck looked so fine that a female penguin left the flock to take a closer look at him. Then she, too, showed off her fine feathers and sleek body. The penguin was very excited. At last he had found a mate.

Four weeks after they had mated, the
female penguin laid a single egg. The
penguins had no nest to keep their egg warm.
So the female carefully passed the precious
egg to her partner. He let her know that he
was ready to take it by making a special call.
Then he lifted a fold of skin above his feet and
tucked the egg under it. He would take care
of the egg from now on.

His mate had nothing left to do, so she set off for the sea. For more than a month she had eaten nothing and she knew there would be nothing to eat now until she reached the sea.

The male penguin had also had nothing to eat. But he had an important job to do and plenty of fat on his body to live on. Even so, guarding the egg was not easy. A great blizzard of snow raged for days on end.

The male penguins shuffled across the ice, balancing their eggs on their feet, fearful lest they roll away. The wind blew, and drifts of snow piled up over their feet and clung to their feathers. The penguins were soon white all over. But their eggs were safe and warm.

The penguin waited on the ice for two long, cold months. Then, one day, the fragile egg shell beneath his feathers broke open and slowly a tiny chick pecked his way out. The little bird sat chirping on his father's feet. He was hungry.

His father was hungry, too. But there was still a little food left in his stomach for the chick. He bent his neck down and the chick reached up inside his bill for the food. Then the two birds waited. The female penguins were coming back from the sea. One by one they arrived, fat and fit, and carrying a cropful of tasty fish.

The penguin watched as the females took over the job of nursing the chicks around him. At last, a plump female waddled towards him. It was his mate. The penguin greeted her with a deep bow. She bent her head towards him and he let the chick shift over to her feet. Then she opened her beak and the chick ate his fill.

The penguin did not stay to watch. He was too hungry. It was time for him and the other males to have something to eat. Standing on the ice for so long had made the penguins tired, hungry and thin. Together they set out for the sea.

Sometimes walking, sometimes sliding on his belly, the penguin struggled towards the fish-filled sea. But the sea was not so far away now. For it was spring and the ice had begun to melt. Soon the penguin saw a seal poking its head through to the air.

Then he saw sheets and chunks of ice floating among clear stretches of water. He was there at last. One by one he and the other penguins reached the sea and dived in. The water was like a warm, silky sheet around his tired body.

The penguin swam far out to sea and ate mouthful after mouthful of fishes and squid. But he did not stay long in the water for his mate and his chick were still on the ice. He stayed only long enough to fatten himself and fill his crop with food. Then he left the water and trailed back across the hard cold ice. It was his turn to nurse the chick while his mate went off to feed.

The chick was soon big enough to leave the comfort of his father's feet. But whenever he left him, he felt cold and frightened, as the wind ruffled his fluffy feathers.

He wanted to snuggle up to the other penguins. But all the others seemed to be huddled together already. He tried to push his way in to the nearest circle of penguin chicks. But they moved even closer together. In the end he went away. As he shuffled off a huge petrel spotted him and swooped down. In terror the tiny penguin flopped down on to his belly and skated to the next huddle.

This time he was lucky. The penguins let him right in to the middle of the huddle. He snuggled up against their soft bodies and felt warm and safe. The petrel circled high above, not daring to attack a whole group of them.

The young penguin stayed with this group all the time from then on. He left them only when his mother or father came back from the sea with fish for him.

The weather grew warmer and the young penguins grew bigger. Soon they would be fully grown and ready to go to sea. But they could not go in the sea with the soft, fluffy feathers they were born with. They needed sleek, strong waterproof feathers.

The young penguin slowly shed his fluffy coat. Soon he was showing off his fine black and white feathers to the others. With this new coat, he was ready to go to sea. He waited until all the others in his huddle were ready, and they all set off together. The last of the adult penguins went too.

For most of the way, all they saw was each other and the sun glinting on the ice. Then the young penguin saw an albatross for the first time. It had swooped down to take a look at the travelers. Other sea birds circled around them, squawking.

The penguins had come to the edge of a low cliff. Below them was the sea. The water looked strange to the young penguin, but the smell that came from the waves made him feel hungry. So he plunged into the water, along with his fellows.

All about him there was food: shoals of silvery fish. The penguins swam after them, enjoying the chase and the tasty meat. They had no idea that other creatures were waiting to taste their flesh.

A leopard seal had been watching from the ice. Now the great creature flopped into the water. The young penguin squawked with terror and he and the others swam for their lives. But it was too late for one of them. The seal's jaws crunched the life from him. The others would make sure to stay away from seals.

The young penguin kept a watch for enemies wherever he swam from then on. As the weeks went by, he became a really good swimmer. Sometimes he left the water to waddle for a while over the ice. But he never went far. He would stay in the sea until winter came. Then, like his father, he would come ashore and trek inland to find a mate.

Penguin Facts

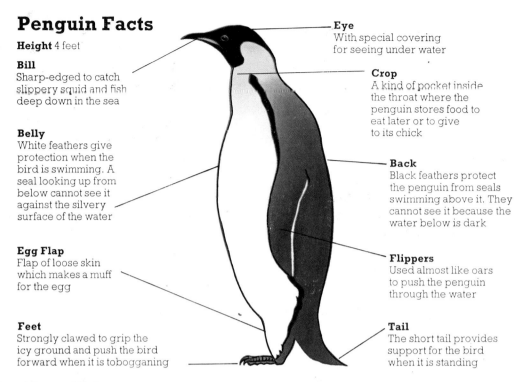

Height 4 feet

Bill
Sharp-edged to catch slippery squid and fish deep down in the sea

Belly
White feathers give protection when the bird is swimming. A seal looking up from below cannot see it against the silvery surface of the water

Egg Flap
Flap of loose skin which makes a muff for the egg

Feet
Strongly clawed to grip the icy ground and push the bird forward when it is tobogganing

Eye
With special covering for seeing under water

Crop
A kind of pocket inside the throat where the penguin stores food to eat later or to give to its chick

Back
Black feathers protect the penguin from seals swimming above it. They cannot see it because the water below is dark

Flippers
Used almost like oars to push the penguin through the water

Tail
The short tail provides support for the bird when it is standing

Wings Under the Water

Penguins are quite unable to fly, but no other bird can match their speed and movement in the water. The penguin's body is perfectly designed for swimming. Penguins often spend many months at sea without ever seeing the land. Their wings have turned into powerful flippers. The way they move up and down makes the penguins seem to fly through the water. The birds can also float on the surface, looking rather like short-necked ducks.

On land, penguins cannot move so well. They stand more or less upright, looking like little men waddling about in evening dress. Because they cannot walk very quickly, they often lie down on their fronts and toboggan over the snow. They push with their feet and flippers.

Keeping Warm

The penguin's body is covered with a thick coat of oily scale-

Five penguin species, including the largest and the smallest. The rockhopper is one of several species with yellow plumes on the head.

Little blue